Facts About the Beaver

By Lisa Strattin

© 2019 Lisa Strattin

FREE BOOK

FREE FOR ALL SUBSCRIBERS

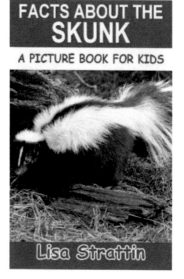

LisaStrattin.com/Subscribe-Here

BOX SET

- FACTS ABOUT THE POISON DART FROGS
- FACTS ABOUT THE THREE TOED SLOTH
- FACTS ABOUT THE RED PANDA
- FACTS ABOUT THE SEAHORSE
- FACTS ABOUT THE PLATYPUS
- FACTS ABOUT THE REINDEER
- FACTS ABOUT THE PANTHER
- FACTS ABOUT THE SIBERIAN HUSKY

LisaStrattin.com/BookBundle

Facts for Kids Picture Books by Lisa Strattin

Little Blue Penguin, Vol 92

Chipmunk, Vol 5

Frilled Lizard, Vol 39

Blue and Gold Macaw, Vol 13

Poison Dart Frogs, Vol 50

Blue Tarantula, Vol 115

African Elephants, Vol 8

Amur Leopard, Vol 89

Sabre Tooth Tiger, Vol 167

Baboon, Vol 174

Sign Up for New Release Emails Here

LisaStrattin.com/subscribe-here

Contents

INTRODUCTION.. 9

CHARACTERISTICS 11

APPEARANCE 13

LIFE STAGES 15

LIFE SPAN 17

SIZE 19

HABITAT... 21

DIET 23

ENEMIES.. 25

SUITABILITY AS PETS.. 27

INTRODUCTION

Beavers are most well known for their distinctive home-building that can be found in rivers and streams. The beavers dam is built from twigs, sticks, leaves and mud and are very strong. They also catch their food there and swim in the water.

CHARACTERISTICS

Beavers are known for the danger signal the beaver makes when startled or frightened. A swimming beaver rapidly dives while slapping the water with its broad tail. This loud slapping noise can be heard over large distances above and below the water. The warning noise serves as an alert to any beavers in the area. Once a beaver makes this signal, nearby beavers dive and may not come back up for some time.

Beavers are slow to move around on land, but they are good swimmers and can stay under water for as long as 15 minutes at a time! In the winter the beaver does not hibernate but instead stores sticks and logs underwater that it can feed on throughout the cold winter.

Beavers have bodies that are made for staying in the water. Their rudder-like tail and webbed feel let them move through the water at 5 miles per hour.

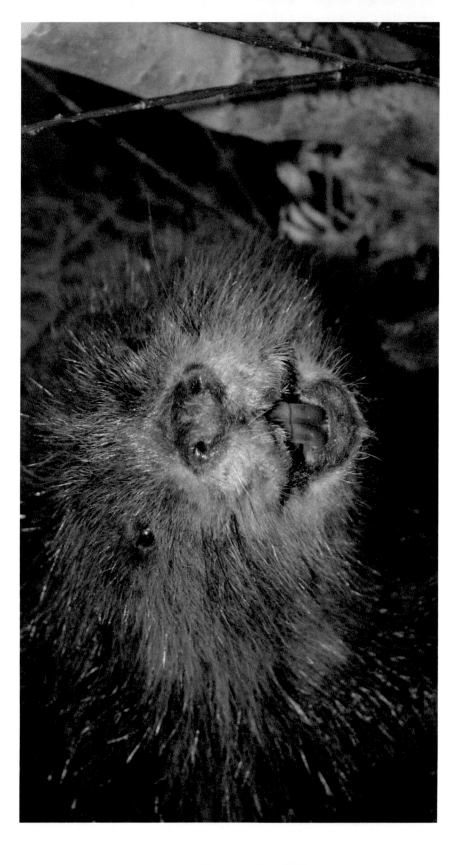

APPEARANCE

A beaver's fur is a rich brown color, and their characteristic flat tail acts as a mechanism to frighten predators away and also as a prop for balance when they are on land. They have continuously growing orange front teeth and their body is a large rounded shape.

Beavers are among the largest living rodents in the world. They have thick fur, webbed feet and flattened, scale-covered tails. With powerful jaws and strong teeth, they fell trees in order to build homes and dams, often changing their environment in ways that few other animals can.

In fact, the phrases "busy as a beaver" and "eager beaver" are synonymous with being industrious and hardworking.

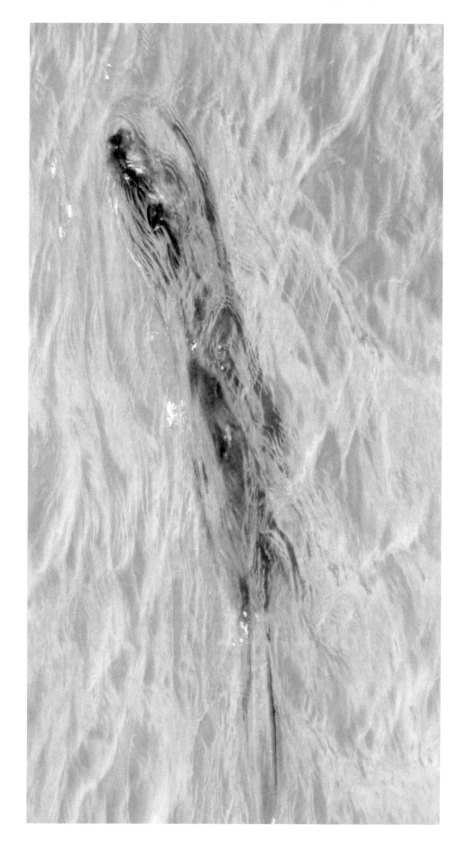

LIFE STAGES

Beavers are very social and live in groups called colonies. Their home is called a lodge and is often the home for one monogamous couple, their young and the yearlings born the year before.

They mate during the winter, from January to March and have an average gestation period of around 100 days. This varies depending on the breed of a particular beaver. Then, they give birth to one to six babies that weigh around 8 to 22 ounces each. Baby beavers are called kits. Eurasian kits are usually weaned after six weeks of life. Beaver kits can swim 24 hours after birth!

At around 2 years of age, the kits leave the lodge and make one of their own. At 3 years old, they begin looking for a mate that they will stay with for their lifetime.

LIFE SPAN

A beaver lives in the wild, for 15 to 20 years.

SIZE

Generally, adult beavers are between 31 and 48 inches long and weigh between 35 to 60 pounds.

HABITAT

All beavers need water to survive. They live in or around freshwater ponds, lakes, rivers, marshes and swamps. American beavers live throughout North America, but stay clear of deserts and the far northern areas of Canada, obviously due to the general lack of water in these regions. Eurasian beavers once lived all over Europe and Asia. Now, they only live in small populations throughout southern Scandinavia, Germany, France, Poland, and central Russia because of hunting.

A beaver's home is called a lodge. These are little dome-shaped houses made from woven sticks, grasses and moss plastered together with mud. They that can be up to 8 feet wide and up to 3 feet high inside. Lodges are built just barely above water level, on the banks of ponds, on islands or on lake shores. Many lodges even have an underwater backdoor for instant swimming access.

DIET

Beavers don't just build homes from trees, they also eat them. Unlike other mammals, beavers digest the cellulose. Beavers also eat leaves, roots and bark from aspens, willows, maples and poplar trees as well as aquatic plants they find in the water.

ENEMIES

Some of the most common predators include fishers, coyotes, hawks, brown and black bears, northern river otters, lynx, eagles, mountain lions, owls, wolverines and wolves. People are also a serious threat to North American beavers, because they are hunted for their skins and fur.

SUITABILITY AS PETS

Beavers are not suitable as a pet. They need to be able to enjoy water and build dams, and this is not something easily provided for them. If you want to see beavers, you might be able to see them at your local zoo or even in the wild if you go camping in areas that they live.

COLOR ME

COLOR ME

COLOR ME

COLOR ME

Please leave me a review here:

LisaStrattin.com/Review-Vol-223

For more Kindle Downloads Visit Lisa Strattin Author Page on Amazon Author Central

amazon.com/author/lisastrattin

To see upcoming titles, visit my website at LisaStrattin.com– most books available on Kindle!

LisaStrattin.com

FREE BOOK

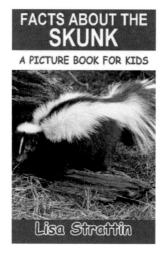

Made in the USA
Middletown, DE
01 December 2021